A Gift for:

_____

From:

_____

Date:

_____

LIVING
praises

Kenneth Boa

COUNTRYMAN

Nashville, Tennessee

To worship

is to quicken the conscience by the holiness of God,

to feed the mind with the truth of God,

to purge the imagination by the beauty of God,

to open up the heart to the love of God,

to devote the will to the purpose of God.

WILLIAM TEMPLE

Introduction

There is no higher calling than to love and worship the infinite and personal God of creation and redemption. A. W. Tozer observed that what comes into our minds when we think about God is the most important thing about us.

Our image of God shapes our spiritual direction and future, and is forged in the times we spend in communion with Him. In complete contrast to the world, God's economy measures greatness not in terms of ability or accomplishments, but in the vitality and integrity of a person's walk with the Lord.

When we take time to meditate on the timeless truths of God's revealed Word, we expand our vision of the living God. In this way we develop a renewed perspective about the things that really matter in this world and in the world to come.

LORD, I PRAISE YOU BECAUSE . . .

You are my strength and my song.

*I will sing to the LORD, for He has triumphed gloriously! . . .
The LORD is my strength and song,
and He has become my salvation;
He is my God, and I will praise Him;
my father's God, and I will exalt Him.*

EXODUS 15:1–2, NKJV

Lord God,

My heart is filled to overflowing with Your praises, for I have seen Your mighty hand at work as You protect me from my enemies. You lift me up with Your outstretched arm and sit me securely in Your presence, high above the problems and circumstances of my everyday life. You are my God and the hope of my life. Therefore, I will praise and worship You with all my heart.

Amen.

LORD, I PRAISE YOU BECAUSE . . .

Your lovingkindness endures forever.

I will give thanks to the LORD, for He is good;
His lovingkindness endures forever. . . .
I will give thanks to the LORD for His unfailing love
and His wonderful acts to the children of men,
for He satisfies the thirsty soul
and fills the hungry soul with good things.

BASED ON PSALM 107:1, 8–9

Dear Lord,

I gratefully acknowledge the blessings of Your faithfulness, goodness, and lovingkindness. Your perfect character never changes, and Your love never fails. You have satisfied my thirsty soul, and You have filled my hungry soul with good things. I thank You for Your wonderful acts on behalf of those who look to You.

Amen.

LORD, I PRAISE YOU BECAUSE . . .

Your faithfulness is everlasting.

Enter into His gates with thanksgiving,
and into His courts with praise.
Be thankful to Him, and bless His name.
For the LORD is good; His mercy is everlasting,
and His truth endures to all generations.

PSALM 100:4–5, NKJV

Lord God,

I will give thanks to You and bless Your name, because
Your faithfulness is everlasting. When I pause and
remember Your many tender mercies, I am filled with
gratitude. May I delight in Your goodness and in
Your faithfulness as I choose to revel in Your presence
and promises rather than dwell on the temporary
problems and setbacks of this life.

Amen.

LORD, I PRAISE YOU BECAUSE . . .

You are great in counsel and mighty in deed.

Oh, Lord GOD, you made the skies and the earth with your
very great power. There is nothing too hard for you to do.
You show love and kindness to thousands of people, but you
also bring punishment to children for their parents' sins.
Great and powerful God, your name is the LORD
All-Powerful. You plan and do great things. You see
everything that people do, and you reward
people for the way they live and for what they do.

JEREMIAH 32:17–19, NCV

14   Week 1, Day 4

Lord God,

When I consider the marvels of the created order, the
wonders of this world, and the awesome expanse of
the heavens, I realize that nothing is too difficult for You.
You are the Lord of hosts, and You know and rule all
things. You are great in counsel and mighty in deed, and
nothing is hidden from Your sight. Therefore I will praise
You and magnify Your name.

Amen.

LORD, I PRAISE YOU BECAUSE . . .

Your right hand is filled with righteousness.

Great is the LORD,
and greatly to be praised in the city of our God,
in His holy mountain. . . .
According to Your name, O God,
so is Your praise to the ends of the earth;
Your right hand is full of righteousness.

PSALM 48:1, 10, NKJV

16   Week 1, Day 5

O God,

You are indeed high and lifted up, and Your greatness exceeds anything my limited mind can imagine. Surely You are most worthy of praise and exaltation and worship, because Your name is holy and awesome. Your right hand is filled with every perfection of goodness, righteousness, and truth.

Amen.

LORD, I PRAISE YOU BECAUSE . . .

You are eternally good.

Oh, give thanks to the LORD, for He is good!
For His mercy endures forever.

PSALM 118:1, NKJV

18   Week 1, Day 6

Lord,

It is with a heart of gratitude and thanksgiving that I approach You. All things come from You, and I acknowledge my utter dependence on You for all that I have, including my very life. You are the supreme good, and Your lovingkindness and mercy on behalf of men and angels are boundless and timeless.

Amen.

LORD, I PRAISE YOU BECAUSE . . .

Your mercies never cease.

But I have hope when I think of this:
The LORD's love never ends;
his mercies never stop.
They are new every morning;
LORD, your loyalty is great.

LAMENTATIONS 3:21–23 NCV

Dear Lord,

Dear Lord

In spite of the sorrows, disappointments, and setbacks in
this life, I know that I can walk in hope because of Your
ceaseless mercies. In Your eternal purposes, You redeem
the things that appear hopeless in this world. Because
Your mercies and compassions never fail, I will declare
Your faithfulness and rejoice in hope.

Amen.

LORD, I PRAISE YOU BECAUSE . . .

Your work is splendid and majestic.

The works of the LORD are great,
studied by all who have pleasure in them.
His work is honorable and glorious,
and His righteousness endures forever.
He has made His wonderful works to be remembered;
the LORD is gracious and full of compassion.

PSALM 111:2–4, NKJV

Lord God,

Your majestic works are evident to the wise and
pondered by those who enjoy them and wonder at them.
Your craftsmanship is splendid and exquisite, and
Your righteousness prevails against all that would rise
up against it. Your acts of grace and compassion are
worthy of all praise and remembrance.

Amen.

LORD, I PRAISE YOU BECAUSE . . .

You have done great things for me.

My soul magnifies the Lord,
and my spirit has rejoiced in God my Savior. . . .
For He who is mighty has done great things for me,
and holy is His name.
And His mercy is on those who fear Him
from generation to generation.

LUKE 1:46–47, 49–50, NKJV

Dear God,

Dear God,

My soul magnifies Your great and holy name, and my
spirit rejoices in acknowledging Your salvation. You are
the Mighty One who has accomplished so many great
and glorious things in the lives of Your people, and Your
holy name is to be extolled and feared in all generations
of Your people.

Amen.

LORD, I PRAISE YOU BECAUSE . . .

Your lovingkindness and faithfulness are ever-present.

It is good to give thanks to the LORD,
and to sing praises to Your name, O Most High;
to declare Your lovingkindness in the morning,
and Your faithfulness every night.

PSALM 92:1–2, NKJV

26   Week 2, Day 4

O Most High,

Your glorious name is honored in heaven and on earth, and I join in the choruses of praise and thanksgiving as I reflect on Your lovingkindness each morning and on Your many acts of faithfulness and tender mercies through the day. You sustain me and give me hope and joy.

Amen.

LORD, I PRAISE YOU BECAUSE . . .

Your ways are righteous and true.

They sing the song of Moses, the servant of God,
and the song of the Lamb, saying:
"Great and marvelous are Your works, Lord God Almighty!
Just and true are Your ways, O King of the saints!
Who shall not fear You, O Lord,
and glorify Your name? For You alone are holy.
For all nations shall come and worship before You,
for Your judgments have been manifested."

REVELATION 15:3–4, NKJV

Lord God Almighty,

I gratefully acknowledge that Your works are great and marvelous, and that Your ways are righteous and true. You are the sovereign Lord of all history and the true King of the nations. Your kingdom alone will prevail, and all knees will bow and acknowledge Your holy name and Your righteous acts.

Amen.

LORD, I PRAISE YOU BECAUSE . . .

You are a righteous God and a Savior.

You, the Lord, alone have declared
what is to come from the distant past.
There is no God apart from You,
a righteous God and a Savior;
there is none besides You.
You are God, and there is no other.

BASED ON ISAIAH 45:21–22

Lord God,

You are the only Savior —holy, pure, altogether lovely, and glorious. There is none besides You, and no person or thing other than You is worthy of worship. In the distant past You revealed that which was to come, and Your promises are sure and steadfast.

Amen.

LORD, I PRAISE YOU BECAUSE . . .

You are the Father of mercies.

Blessed be the God and Father of our Lord Jesus Christ,
the Father of mercies and God of all comfort.

2 CORINTHIANS 1:3, NKJV

Father of our Lord Jesus Christ,

It gives me great encouragement to know that You are the Father of mercies and the God of all comfort. Because of Your good, loving, and unchanging character, I can wholly trust in Your promises and in the timeless truths of Your Word.

Amen.

LORD, I PRAISE YOU BECAUSE . . .

You are the everlasting God.

Lord, you have been our home since the beginning.
Before the mountains were born and before you created
the earth and the world, you are God.
You have always been, and you will always be.
You turn people back into dust.
You say, "Go back into dust, human beings."
To you, a thousand years is like the passing of
a day, or like a few hours in the night.

PSALM 90:1–4, NCV

Lord,

I marvel at the concept of Your eternality—You are the uncaused I AM THAT I AM whose nature is always to exist. From everlasting to everlasting, You always are, inhabiting Your temporal creation, but not limited to it. By contrast, my years on this earth are but a tiny moment. Yet You have given me the hope of everlasting life through Christ who now indwells me.

Amen.

LORD, I PRAISE YOU BECAUSE . . .

Your power and understanding are boundless.

God, the Holy One, says,
"Can you compare me to anyone? Is anyone equal to me?"
Look up to the skies. Who created all these stars?
He leads out the army of heaven one by one
and calls all the stars by name.
Because he is strong and powerful, not one of them is missing. . . .
Surely you know. Surely you have heard.
The LORD is the God who lives forever, who created all the world.
He does not become tired or need to rest.
No one can understand how great his wisdom is.

ISAIAH 40:25–26, 28, NCV

Everlasting God,

No one can compare with You, the infinite and personal
creator of the heavens and the earth. You spoke the vast
array of stars into being and know them each by name,
though their number is stupendous. You order and control
all things through Your sovereign power, and nothing
escapes Your lordship. You rule all things in Your universe,
and I can trust You to order my life as well.

Amen.

LORD, I PRAISE YOU BECAUSE . . .

Your years will have no end.

My days are like a lengthened shadow,
and I wither away like grass.
But You, O LORD, will endure forever,
and the remembrance of Your name to all generations.
Of old, You laid the foundations of the earth,
and the heavens are the work of Your hands.
They will perish, but You will endure;
they will all wear out like a garment.
Like clothing, You will change them,
and they will be discarded.
But You are the same, and Your years will have no end.

BASED ON PSALM 102:11–12, 25–27

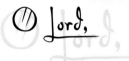

O Lord,

Though all things in this created order are subject to change and decay, You never change, and Your power and years are never diminished. You who laid the foundations of the earth and spoke the heavens into being also will create new heavens and a new earth that will endure.

Amen.

LORD, I PRAISE YOU BECAUSE . . .

*You rule over all the kingdoms
of the nations.*

LORD, God of our ancestors,
you are the God in heaven.
You rule over all the kingdoms of the nations.
You have power and strength,
so no one can stand against you.

2 CHRONICLES 20:6, NCV

God of all,

You are the ruler over all the kingdoms of the nations.
You raise up and depose the kingdoms of this earth—only
Your kingdom is everlasting. Nothing can thwart Your
good and perfect purposes, for You alone are the God of
heaven. I delight in Your power, in Your sovereign rule,
and in Your loving purposes for those whose hearts are
fixed on You.

Amen.

LORD, I PRAISE YOU BECAUSE . . .

You are the God of our salvation.

By awesome deeds in righteousness
You will answer us, O God of our salvation,
You who are the confidence of all the ends of the earth,
and of the far-off seas;
Who established the mountains by His strength,
being clothed with power;
You who still the noise of the seas, the noise of their waves,
and the tumult of the peoples.

PSALM 65:5–7, NKJV

God of my salvation,

God of my salvation,

I rejoice in Your awesome deeds of righteousness.
The whole creation from the scale of the smallest
to the greatest is filled with the evidences of Your
magnificent beauty, glory, and boundless creativity.
You have made all things well, and Your power is
evident everywhere I look. May I walk in humility
and gratitude before You, the God of my salvation.

Amen.

LORD, I PRAISE YOU BECAUSE . . .

You are exalted on high.

From the rising of the sun to its going down
the LORD's name is to be praised.
The LORD is high above all nations,
His glory above the heavens.
Who is like the LORD our God,
who dwells on high, who humbles Himself
to behold the things that are in the heavens and in the earth?

PSALM 113:3–6, NKJV

Lord God,

You are the One who is enthroned on high, and Your glorious name is to be praised and exalted. Your majesty and splendor transcend all things, and yet You have humbled Yourself to behold and to be concerned with the things that are in the heavens and in the earth. In light of this, I marvel at the meaning of the incarnation of Your Son and at the suffering He bore to purchase our salvation.

Amen.

LORD, I PRAISE YOU BECAUSE . . .

You rule over all Your creation.

The Lord GOD All–Powerful touches the land,
and the land shakes. Then everyone who lives in
the land cries for the dead. The whole land
rises like the Nile River and falls like the river of
Egypt. The LORD builds his upper rooms
above the skies; he sets their foundations on the earth.
He calls for the waters of the sea and
pours them out on the land. The LORD is his name.

AMOS 9:5–6, NCV

Lord God of hosts,

The glories of the heavens and of the earth all point
to You. Your authority and power are evident in the
sea and in the sky, in the sun and moon and the starry
hosts in the vast expanse of space. All these are in
Your hands, and nothing can defeat Your purposes that
You planned from before the foundation of the earth,
even from all eternity.

Amen.

LORD, I PRAISE YOU BECAUSE . . .

Your dominion endures through all generations.

All Your works shall praise You, O LORD,
and Your saints shall bless You.
They shall speak of the glory of Your kingdom,
and talk of Your power,
to make known to the sons of men His mighty acts,
and the glorious majesty of His kingdom.
Your kingdom is an everlasting kingdom,
and Your dominion endures throughout all generations.

PSALM 145:10–13, NKJV

48   Week 4, Day 3

O Lord,

Though the kingdoms and works of this earth all perish,
Your kingdom and mighty works will endure forever.
I rejoice in Your dominion that endures through all
generations and in the glorious majesty of Your kingdom.
May I speak of Your glory and of Your power, and may I
magnify Your glorious name forever!

Amen.

LORD, I PRAISE YOU BECAUSE . . .

You give all men life and breath.

God, who made the world and everything in it,
since He is Lord of heaven and earth,
does not dwell in temples made with hands.
Nor is He worshipped with men's hands,
as though He needed anything,
since He gives to all life, breath, and all things.

ACTS 17:24–25, NKJV

Lord God,

You are Lord of the entire cosmos. You made the world and everything in it, and You sustain Your creatures by giving them life and breath and providing for their needs. You have no needs, but You choose to want us and to love us. May I worship You in Spirit and in truth, glorifying Your holy name in the beauty of holiness.

Amen.

LORD, I PRAISE YOU BECAUSE . . .

You created all things and sustain them.

No one can see God, but Jesus Christ is exactly like him.
He ranks higher than everything that has been made.
Through his power all things were made—things in heaven
and on earth, things seen and unseen, all powers,
authorities, lords, and rulers. All things were made through
Christ and for Christ. He was there before anything was
made, and all things continue because of him.

COLOSSIANS 1:15–17, NCV

Lord Christ,

You created all things in heaven and on earth. All
things come from You and for You, and You are before
all things. Your dominion extends from the heavens
to the earth, and from the visible to the invisible. All
angelic beings are under Your divine authority, and
Your kingdom is everlasting.

Amen.

LORD, I PRAISE YOU BECAUSE . . .

You are gracious and compassionate.

I will express the memory of Your abundant goodness
and joyfully sing of Your righteousness.
The LORD is gracious and compassionate,
slow to anger, and great in lovingkindness.
The LORD is good to all,
and His tender mercies are over all His works.

BASED ON PSALM 145:7–9

54   Week 4, Day 6

Lord,

I praise You because You are gracious and compassionate. Your patience and lovingkindness are wonderful, and Your goodness extends to all who seek You. I thank You for Your many tender mercies that are so evident in my life. When I reflect upon them, I realize that they extend to many things for which I have not been grateful. I will rejoice in Your righteousness and lift up Your holy name.

Amen.

LORD, I PRAISE YOU BECAUSE . . .

You created all things.

You are worthy, O Lord,
to receive glory and honor and power;
for You created all things,
and by Your will they exist and were created.

REVELATION 4:11, NKJV

Lord and God,

It is my pleasure to exalt and lift up Your great and
marvelous name, for You alone are worthy to receive
glory and honor and power. All things derive their
being from You, and You order and sustain the universe.
I will rejoice in Your perfections and powers and delight
in the boundless wealth of Your goodness and love.

Amen.

LORD, I PRAISE YOU BECAUSE . . .

You keep Your covenant and mercy with Your people.

O LORD, God of Israel, there is no God like You
in heaven above or on earth below;
You keep Your covenant and mercy
with Your servants who
walk before You with all their hearts.

BASED ON 1 KINGS 8:23 & 2 CHRONICLES 6:14

O Lord,

You are beyond human comprehension, and yet You
delight to commune with Your people. You have
entered into a covenant relationship with those who
know You, and Your mercy and grace extend into
every facet of our lives. As Your loving servant, may
I walk before You with all my heart and honor Your
perfect name.

Amen.

LORD, I PRAISE YOU BECAUSE . . .

You will judge the world in righteousness.

But the LORD rules forever.
He sits on his throne to judge,
and he will judge the world in fairness;
he will decide what is fair for the nations.
The LORD defends those who suffer;
he defends them in times of trouble.
Those who know the LORD trust him,
because he will not leave those who come to him.

PSALM 9:7–10, NCV

Lord God,

You are my sure refuge and stronghold in times of
trouble. I can fully trust in You and look to You when
I am distressed and cast down. You are the fountainhead
of righteousness, justice, mercy, goodness, and grace,
and You will not forsake those who seek You. Because
of Your wonderful character and ways, I will praise
and exalt Your name forever.

Amen.

LORD, I PRAISE YOU BECAUSE . . .

Your holiness is beautiful.

For the LORD is great and greatly to be praised;
He is also to be feared above all gods.
For all the gods of the peoples are idols,
but the LORD made the heavens.
Honor and majesty are before Him;
strength and gladness are in His place.
Give to the LORD, O families of the peoples,
give to the LORD glory and strength.
Give to the LORD the glory due His name;
bring an offering, and come before Him.
Oh, worship the LORD in the beauty of holiness!

1 CHRONICLES 16:25–29, NKJV

Week 5, Day 1

Dear Lord,

Dear Lord,

The beauty of Your holiness is beyond all mortal comprehension. It is evident in Your creation, and in Your Word, and in the person and work of Your Son. I praise Your greatness, Your splendor, Your majesty, Your strength, Your joy, and Your glory. I will acknowledge the glory due Your name and worship You in the beauty of holiness.

Amen.

LORD, I PRAISE YOU BECAUSE . . .

You rise to show compassion.

The LORD wants to show his mercy to you.
He wants to rise and comfort you.
The LORD is a fair God,
and everyone who waits for his help will be happy.

ISAIAH 30:18, NCV

Lord God,

You are the absolute and perfect and unchanging source of goodness and justice. Your grace permeates Your words and Your works and Your ways. I will wait upon You, rest in You, trust in You, and commit my ways to You. You richly bless all who call upon Your name in humility and expectation and hope.

Amen.

LORD, I PRAISE YOU BECAUSE . . .

You uphold all things by Your powerful word.

The Son reflects the glory of God
and shows exactly what God is like.
He holds everything together with his powerful word.
When the Son made people clean from their sins,
he sat down at the right side of God, the Great One in heaven.
The Son became much greater than the angels,
and God gave him a name that is much greater than theirs.

HEBREWS 1:3–4, NCV

Lord Jesus,

You radiate God's glory as the exact representation of His being. To see You is to see the Father, and to hear Your words is to listen to the voice of the Father. You who uphold all things by the word of Your power came down from heaven to cleanse us of our sins. You are seated at the right hand of the Majesty on high, and You are worshiped with the Father and with the Holy Spirit.

Amen.

LORD, I PRAISE YOU BECAUSE . . .

You humble and You exalt.

The LORD brings death and makes alive;
He brings down to the grave and raises up.
The LORD sends poverty and wealth;
He humbles and He exalts.
He raises the poor from the dust
and lifts the needy from the ash heap,
to seat them with princes
and make them inherit a throne of honor.
For the foundations of the earth are the LORD's,
and He has set the world upon them.

BASED ON 1 SAMUEL 2:6–8

Lord,

You established the foundations of the earth, and
You have determined our appointed times and the
boundaries of our habitations. Our lives are in Your
hand, and it is in Your sovereign counsel to raise up
or depose, to exalt or humble, to give wealth or
poverty. You alone know what is best for Your people,
and You alone have the power to bring it about.

Amen.

LORD, I PRAISE YOU BECAUSE . . .

You are the high and lofty One.

And this is the reason: God lives forever and is holy.
He is high and lifted up. He says, I live in a high
and holy place, but I also live with people who are sad
and humble. I give new life to those who
are humble and to those whose hearts are broken.

ISAIAH 57:15, NCV

Father in the heavenlies,

Father in the heavenlies,

You inhabit eternity, and Your years have no beginning or end. You dwell in exalted majesty and in unimaginable holiness. And yet You have chosen to be close to those who are contrite and lowly in spirit and to revive their hearts and spirits as they look to You, hope in You, and wait upon You.

Amen.

LORD, I PRAISE YOU BECAUSE . . .

You fulfill the desire of those who fear You.

The LORD is near to all who call upon Him,
to all who call upon Him in truth.
He will fulfill the desire of those who fear Him;
He also will hear their cry and save them.
The LORD preserves all who love Him,
but all the wicked He will destroy.

PSALM 145:18–20, NKJV

Lord,

I give thanks that You are indeed near to all who call upon You in truth. You satisfy the desire of all who look to You and trust in You and who fear Your holy name. You are the Savior and preserver of all who love You. You hold and protect Your people and keep them from destruction. I will hope in You and rejoice in Your salvation.

Amen.

LORD, I PRAISE YOU BECAUSE . . .

You are in authority over all of human affairs.

Blessed be the name of God forever and ever,
for wisdom and might are His.
And He changes the times and the seasons;
He removes kings and raises up kings;
He gives wisdom to the wise
and knowledge to those who have understanding.
He reveals deep and secret things;
He knows what is in the darkness,
and light dwells with Him.

DANIEL 2:20–22, NKJV

74   Week 6, Day 4

Lord God,

All might, power, rule, dominion, and authority is Yours, holy God. I lift up Your great and glorious name and walk in amazement at Your goodness and grace. You rule over the affairs of men and nations, and You are the source of wisdom, knowledge, and understanding. You dwell in inapproachable light, and nothing is hidden from Your omniscient view.

Amen.

LORD, I PRAISE YOU BECAUSE . . .

You have done wonderful things.

LORD, you are my God.
I honor you and praise you,
because you have done amazing things.
You have always done what you said you would do;
you have done what you planned long ago.

ISAIAH 25:1, NCV

O Lord,

Even before the foundation of the earth, You chose
Your people and called them to dwell with You
in the joy and glory of holiness. Your wonders are
inexhaustible, and Your councils are inscrutable.
Who can grasp the fullness of Your will and Your
ways? I will exalt You and praise Your holy name.

Amen.

LORD, I PRAISE YOU BECAUSE . . .

You delight to show mercy and forgiveness.

Who is a God like You, who pardons iniquity
and passes over the transgression of the
remnant of His inheritance?
You do not stay angry forever
but delight to show mercy.
You will have compassion on Your people;
You will tread their iniquities underfoot
and hurl all their sins into the depths of the sea.

BASED ON MICAH 7:18–19

Lord God,

There is no one like You—glorious in might and authority, You also dwell with the lowly and delight to bestow mercy upon them. In Your great compassion, You overcome our iniquities and completely remove our transgressions. I rejoice in Your wonderful compassion, because it is the source of my life and hope.

Amen.

LORD, I PRAISE YOU BECAUSE . . .

You reveal Yourself to those You have chosen.

Jesus rejoiced in the Holy Spirit, and said,
"I praise You, Father, Lord of heaven and earth,
because You have hidden these things from the wise and learned,
and revealed them to little children.
Yes, Father, for this was well–pleasing in Your sight.
All things have been delivered to Me by My Father.
No one knows the Son except the Father,
and no one knows the Father except the Son
and those to whom the Son chooses to reveal Him."

BASED ON MATTHEW 11:25–27 & LUKE 10:21–22

Father,

I rejoice with Your Son and Your Holy Spirit in Your perfect wisdom. For You chose to reveal Your truth to those who approach You with the trust and humility of little children. I could never hope to know You unless the Son had chosen to reveal You to me. The Lord Jesus is my life and hope, and I give You thanks and praise that He came down from heaven.

Amen.

LORD, I PRAISE YOU BECAUSE . . .

You gave Yourself for our sins.

Grace and peace to you from God our Father
and the Lord Jesus Christ. Jesus gave
himself for our sins to free us from this evil world
we live in, as God the Father planned.
The glory belongs to God forever and ever. Amen.

GALATIANS 1:3–5, NCV

Lord Jesus,

You are my light and my salvation, and I will always hope and trust in You. For You gave Yourself for my sins to rescue me from the present evil age and to grant me the joy of Your presence in the ages to come. All glory is Yours, both now and forever. You are the Alpha and the Omega, the First and the Last, the Beginning and the End.

Amen.

LORD, I PRAISE YOU BECAUSE . . .

You are great, and Your name is mighty in power.

LORD, there is no one like you. You are great,
and your name is great and powerful. Everyone should
respect you, King of the nations; you deserve respect.
Of all the wise people among the nations
and in all the kingdoms, none of them is as wise as you.

JEREMIAH 10:6–7, NCV

King of the nations,

Your great and glorious name is to be lifted up and
magnified in all times and places, because it is Your
rightful due. The rulers and authorities of this earth
come and go, and their kingdoms last but for a moment
before they disappear. But You inhabit all ages and
are Lord of all that is on the earth and in the heavens.
There is no one like You.

Amen.

LORD, I PRAISE YOU BECAUSE . . .

You have visited and redeemed Your people.

Blessed is the Lord God of Israel,
For He has visited and redeemed His people,
And has raised up a horn of salvation for us
In the house of His servant David,
As He spoke by the mouth of His holy prophets,
Who have been since the world began,
That we should be saved from our enemies
And from the hand of all who hate us,
To perform the mercy promised to our fathers
And to remember His holy covenant,
The oath which He swore to our father Abraham:
To grant us that we, being delivered
from the hand of our enemies, might serve Him without fear,
In holiness and righteousness before Him all the days of our life.
LUKE 1:68–75, NKJV

Lord God,

It is my honor and joy to serve You without fear, in holiness and righteousness before You all my days. You are the Author of our salvation and the Keeper of the covenant promises You have made through Your servants the prophets. You have redeemed Your people through the blood of the new covenant that was shed for us. Therefore I will bless and glorify Your great name forever.

Amen.

LORD, I PRAISE YOU BECAUSE . . .

You empower those who have trusted in You.

And you will know that God's power is very great
for us who believe. That power is the same as the
great strength God used to raise Christ from the dead
and put him at his right side in the heavenly world.
God has put Christ over all rulers, authorities, powers,
and kings, not only in this world but also in the next.

EPHESIANS 1:19–21, NCV

Dear God,

You exerted Your mighty strength when You raised Christ Jesus from the dead and seated Him at Your right hand in the heavenly places. You exalted Him far above all rule and authority and above all earthly and heavenly powers to a glorious dominion that will never end. I praise You that this same power works in my life because of my identification with Jesus in His death, burial, resurrection, and ascension.

Amen.

LORD, I PRAISE YOU BECAUSE . . .

You are the First and the Last.

When I saw him, I fell down at his feet like a dead man.
He put his right hand on me and said, "Do not be afraid.
I am the First and the Last. I am the One who lives;
I was dead, but look, I am alive forever and ever!
And I hold the keys to death and to the place of the dead."

REVELATION 1:17–18, NCV

Lord, Jesus,

You are the First and the Last, the Living One who
has defeated death and holds the keys of death and of
life. Your death brought about the death of death,
and Your resurrection is the basis for our resurrection
life. You have redeemed Your people—body, soul,
and spirit—and they will be coheirs with You in the
heavenly places in the ages to come.

Amen.

LORD, I PRAISE YOU BECAUSE . . .

You have shown Your greatness and Your mighty deeds.

Lord GOD, you have begun to show me,
your servant, how great you are.
You have great strength,
and no other god in heaven or on earth
can do the powerful things you do.
There is no other god like you.

DEUTERONOMY 3:24, NCV

O Lord God,

You are utterly unique, magnificent, incomprehensible,
transcendent, majestic, holy, glorious, righteous, perfect,
and powerful. You dwell in the beauty of holiness and
in the splendor of majesty, and nothing in all creation is
like You, for You alone created all things for Your glory
and good pleasure.

Amen.

LORD, I PRAISE YOU BECAUSE . . .

You purchased us with Your blood.

And they sang a new song, saying:
"You are worthy to take the scroll,
And to open its seals;
For You were slain,
And have redeemed us to God by Your blood
Out of every tribe and tongue and people and nation,
And have made us kings and priests to our God;
And we shall reign on the earth."

REVELATION 5:9–10, NKJV

Lord Jesus,

I exalt You and praise Your holy name for purchasing men for God from every tribe and language and people and nation with Your blood. It was Your good pleasure to call them to be a kingdom and priests to serve the living God. You are worthy of all honor and praise, and it is my joy and delight to call to mind Your perfections and goodness.

Amen.

LORD, I PRAISE YOU BECAUSE . . .

Your kingdom will endure forever.

He will be great,
and will be called the Son of the Highest;
and the Lord God will give Him
the throne of His father David.
And He will reign over the house of Jacob forever,
and of His kingdom there will be no end.

LUKE 1:32–33, NKJV

Lord Jesus,

You are the Messiah, the anointed One, the fulfillment
of the promises made by Your prophets in the law, the
prophets, and the writings. All Scripture speaks of You
and points to Your work as prophet, priest, and king.
You will inherit the throne of David and reign over the
earth in righteousness, justice, and truth.

Amen.

LORD, I PRAISE YOU BECAUSE . . .

You gave Yourself to redeem us from all iniquity.

We are looking for the blessed hope and the glorious appearing
of our great God and Savior, Christ Jesus,
who gave Himself for us to redeem us from all iniquity
and to purify for Himself a people for His own possession,
zealous for good works.

BASED ON TITUS 2:13–14

Lord Jesus,

You are our great God and Savior, and I wait with
expectant and blessed hope for Your glorious appearing.
In Your love and obedience to the will of the Father,
You gave Yourself for us to redeem us from all iniquity.
I praise You that You have called me to be part of a
people for Your own possession, zealous for good works.

Amen.

LORD, I PRAISE YOU BECAUSE . . .

You are worthy of all honor and
glory and blessing.

Then I looked, and I heard the voice of many angels
around the throne, the living creatures, and the elders; and
the number of them was ten thousand times ten thousand,
and thousands of thousands, saying with a loud voice:
"Worthy is the Lamb who was slain
To receive power and riches and wisdom,
And strength and honor and glory and blessing!"

REVELATION 5:11–12, NKJV

Lord Jesus,

You are the Passover Lamb of God who takes away
the sins of the world. You humbled Yourself to the point
of death on the cross, and You have been exalted to
receive power and riches and wisdom and strength and
honor and glory and blessing. The whole host of heaven
praises You, and it is my delight to join the praises of
this glorious throng.

Amen.

LORD, I PRAISE YOU BECAUSE . . .

Your name will be great among the nations.

"From the east to the west I will be honored
among the nations. Everywhere they will bring incense
and clean offerings to me, because I will be
honored among the nations," says the LORD All-Powerful.

MALACHI 1:11, NCV

Lord God,

Your name is great and wondrous, and it is to be
exalted among the nations. The day will come when
You return and Your will is done on earth as it is in
heaven. All nations will honor the Lord Jesus, and
He will reign on the throne of David. I worship You—
Father, Son, and Holy Spirit—and rejoice in Your
glory and Your salvation.

Amen.

LORD, I PRAISE YOU BECAUSE . . .

You have bestowed Your grace upon us.

God chose me in Christ before the foundation of the world
to be holy and blameless in His sight.
In love He predestined me to be adopted as His child
through Jesus Christ,
according to the good pleasure of His will,
to the praise of the glory of His grace,
which He bestowed upon me in the One He loves.

BASED ON EPHESIANS 1:4–6

Father,

I give thanks that in Your great love You chose me even before the foundation of the world to be Your adopted child through Your Son Jesus Christ. This was according to the good pleasure of Your will and to the praise of the glory of Your grace, which You bestowed upon me in Him. I rejoice that I have been embraced by Your love.

Amen.

LORD, I PRAISE YOU BECAUSE . . .

You are compassionate and gracious.

The LORD passed in front of Moses, and said, "I am the LORD. The LORD is a God who shows mercy, who is kind, who doesn't become angry quickly, who has great love and faithfulness and is kind to thousands of people. The LORD forgives people for evil, for sin, and for turning against him, but he does not forget to punish guilty people."

EXODUS 34:6–7, NCV

Lord God,

I stand amazed at the beauty of Your attributes: Your
perfect compassion, Your boundless grace, Your infinite
patience, Your abundant lovingkindness, Your wonderful
truth, Your intense love, and Your wonderful forgiveness.
Because of who You are, I can walk in faith, hope,
and love.

Amen.

LORD, I PRAISE YOU BECAUSE . . .

You are the King eternal, immortal, invisible.

Now to the King eternal, immortal, invisible, to God who alone is wise, be honor and glory forever and ever. Amen.

1 TIMOTHY 1:17, NKJV

O Lord my King,

In Your essence You are incomprehensible and
mysterious. You have revealed that You are eternal,
immortal, and invisible, and Your transcendent
majesty is boundless. And yet You choose to want us
for Yourself and give us the gift of Your indwelling
Spirit. To You be honor and glory forever and ever.

Amen.

LORD, I PRAISE YOU BECAUSE . . .

You are mighty and awesome.

For the LORD your God is God of gods and
Lord of lords, the great God, mighty and awesome,
who shows no partiality nor takes a bribe.
He administers justice for the fatherless and the widow,
and loves the stranger, giving him food and clothing.

DEUTERONOMY 10:17–18, NKJV

O Lord my God,

You are the mighty and awesome God of gods and Lord of lords. I praise You that You show no partiality and accept no bribes, but that You execute justice for those who are in need. My hope is fixed on Your unchanging character and on Your gracious promises, and I give thanks for who You are.

Amen.

LORD, I PRAISE YOU BECAUSE . . .

You are the author of our salvation.

*After the vision of these things I looked, and there was
a great number of people, so many that no one
could count them. They were from every nation, tribe,
people, and language of the earth. They were all
standing before the throne and before the Lamb, wearing
white robes and holding palm branches in their hands.
They were shouting in a loud voice, "Salvation belongs to
our God, who sits on the throne, and to the Lamb."*

REVELATION 7:9–10, NCV

Lord God,

Salvation belongs to the triune God—Father, Son, and Holy Spirit. You chose us for Yourself, redeemed us with the blood of Christ, and regenerated us through the power of Your Holy Spirit. You are to be exalted and magnified by the great host of Your creatures because of who You are and what You have done.

Amen.

LORD, I PRAISE YOU BECAUSE . . .

Your righteousness and wonders are measureless.

My mouth shall tell of Your righteousness
And Your salvation all the day,
For I do not know their limits.
I will go in the strength of the Lord GOD;
I will make mention of Your righteousness, of Yours only.
O God, You have taught me from my youth;
And to this day I declare Your wondrous works.

PSALM 71:15–17, NKJV

O God,

I will rejoice and exult in Your righteousness, a
righteousness that is perfect, holy, pure, good,
loving, patient, just, compassionate, and altogether
lovely. It is through Your salvation that I have
meaning and hope in this world, and Your presence
is ever with me. It is Your strength that sustains me,
and I will proclaim Your measureless righteousness
and salvation to the glory of Your name.

Amen.

LORD, I PRAISE YOU BECAUSE . . .

You love me and protect me.

Who shall separate me from the love of Christ?
Shall tribulation, or distress, or persecution,
or famine, or nakedness, or danger, or sword?
As it is written: "For Your sake we face death all day long;
we are considered as sheep to be slaughtered."
Yet in all these things I am more than a conqueror
through Him who loved me.

BASED ON ROMANS 8:35–37

Lord Jesus,

Nothing at all can separate me from Your causeless, measureless, and ceaseless love. No person or force in heaven, on earth, or under the earth can remove me from Your loving grip, for You are Lord of all. In spite of the afflictions, adversities, setbacks, and uncertainties of this earthly life, I am secure in You.

Amen.

LORD, I PRAISE YOU BECAUSE . . .

You are worthy of glory,
majesty, dominion, and authority.

To God our Savior,
Who alone is wise,
Be glory and majesty,
Dominion and power,
Both now and forever.
Amen.

JUDE 25, NKJV

Lord God,

You are the only God and Savior, and Jesus Christ is the
glorious King of kings and Lord of lords who purchased
us and liberated us from our bondage to sin and death.
All glory, majesty, dominion, and authority are Yours,
O Lord, before all ages, now, and forever.

Amen.

LORD, I PRAISE YOU BECAUSE . . .

Your dominion is an eternal dominion.

The Most High is sovereign over the kingdoms of men
and gives them to whomever He wishes. . . .
I will bless the Most High
and praise and honor Him who lives forever.
His dominion is an eternal dominion,
and His kingdom endures from generation to generation.
He regards all the inhabitants of the earth as nothing,
and does as He pleases with the host of heaven
and the inhabitants of the earth.
No one can hold back His hand or say to Him:
"What have You done?" . . .
I praise, exalt, and honor the King of heaven,
for all His works are true, and all His ways are just,
and He is able to humble those who walk in pride.

BASED ON DANIEL 4:17, 34–35, 37

God Most High,

I will bless and honor You, the Most High who lives forever. You rule in the splendor of sovereignty over all kingdoms and all creation, and Your dominion is everlasting. You do all that You please with the host of heaven and the inhabitants of the earth, and all Your works are true and Your ways just. Your name is praised above all.

Amen.

LORD, I PRAISE YOU BECAUSE . . .

You are exalted as head over all.

LORD, you are great and powerful. You have glory,
victory, and honor. Everything in heaven and
on earth belongs to you. The kingdom belongs to
you, LORD; you are the ruler over everything.
Riches and honor come from you. You rule everything.
You have the power and strength to make anyone
great and strong. Now, our God, we thank you and
praise your glorious name. These things did not
really come from me and my people. Everything comes
from you; we have given you back what you gave us.

1 CHRONICLES 29:11–14, NCV

O Lord,

You are exalted as head over all things, and it is from Your hand that every good gift is given. You are awesome in power and in might, and all greatness, glory, victory, and majesty are Yours, O Lord. I give You thanks and bless and praise Your glorious name. All that I am and have comes from You, and I offer myself to You as a living sacrifice.

Amen.

LORD, I PRAISE YOU BECAUSE . . .

You will treasure Your servants forever.

Nothing that God judges guilty will be in that city.
The throne of God and of the Lamb will be there, and God's
servants will worship him. They will see his face,
and his name will be written on their foreheads. There will
never be night again. They will not need the light of a
lamp or the light of the sun, because the Lord God will give
them light. And they will rule as kings forever and ever.

REVELATION 22:3–5, NCV

Lord God,

Lord God,

I look with great anticipation at the promise of Your
heavenly kingdom in which there will be no night, no
curse, no death, no sickness, no mourning, and no
crying. You will make all things new, and we will behold
the light and beauty of Your face. I praise You for
the hope of heaven and the glories of the age to come.

Amen.

LORD, I PRAISE YOU BECAUSE . . .

You have clothed me with the garments of salvation.

I will greatly rejoice in the LORD,
My soul shall be joyful in my God;
For He has clothed me with the garments of salvation,
He has covered me with the robe of righteousness,
As a bridegroom decks himself with ornaments,
And as a bride adorns herself with her jewels.

ISAIAH 61:10, NKJV

Lord God,

I bless and exalt Your high, majestic, wonderful,
awesome, and holy name. My soul will rejoice in
the Lord who has clothed me with the garments of
salvation. You have arrayed me in the robe of the
righteousness of Christ, and You have blessed me
with His indwelling life. I praise You that You will
come again and receive me to Yourself, so that
where You are, there I will be also.

Amen.

Kenneth Boa is engaged in a ministry of relational evangelism and discipleship, teaching, writing, and speaking. He holds a B.S. from Case Institute of Technology, a Th.M. from Dallas Theological Seminary, a Ph.D. from New York University, and a D.Phil. from the University of Oxford in England.

He is the President of Reflections Ministries, an organization that seeks to encourage, teach, and equip people to know Christ, follow Him, become progressively conformed to His image, and reproduce His life in others.

Dr. Boa writes a free monthly teaching letter called *Reflections*. If you would like to be on the mailing list, visit www.reflectionsministries.org or call 800–DRAW NEAR (800–372–9632).